POOKA AND THE LITTLE BLUE EGG

POOKA WAS SITTING UNDER A TREE.
CUCKOO! CUCKOO!

THUD!
A speckled egg shiny and blue, landed on the
ground.

"AH ooh!" said Pooka, he scratched his head , puzzled by what he'd found. He picked it up and folded it into a big crinkled dock leaf that was growing nearby and he made a sack big and round. Now he could carry the egg safely on his back because he didn't want it to go KER-ACK!.

Off he set with the egg in the leaf sack on his back to find someone who knew where the speckled egg, shiny and blue maybe grew.

Up hill and down dale he trotted until he came to a stream he had to leap across.

He landed right in front of Mrs Frog all green and spotted.

"What do you have in that sack on your back?" she said

"A speckled egg, shiny and blue. Is it yours ? Is this where it grew?" said Pooka

"Ribbitt, ribbitt, no.
My eggs are in the water, safe in a big bunch of jelly, just in case anyone wants them for lunch to fill their belly." said Mrs Frog.

Pooka went on his way, following the bubbling stream until he came to deep green river. He couldn't get round it so he decided to swim across it,. The cold water made him shiver.

Mrs Trout came swimming up and said with a splish and a shout.

"What do you have in that sack on your back?"

"A speckled egg, shiny and blue. Is it yours? Is this where it grew? Said Pooka.

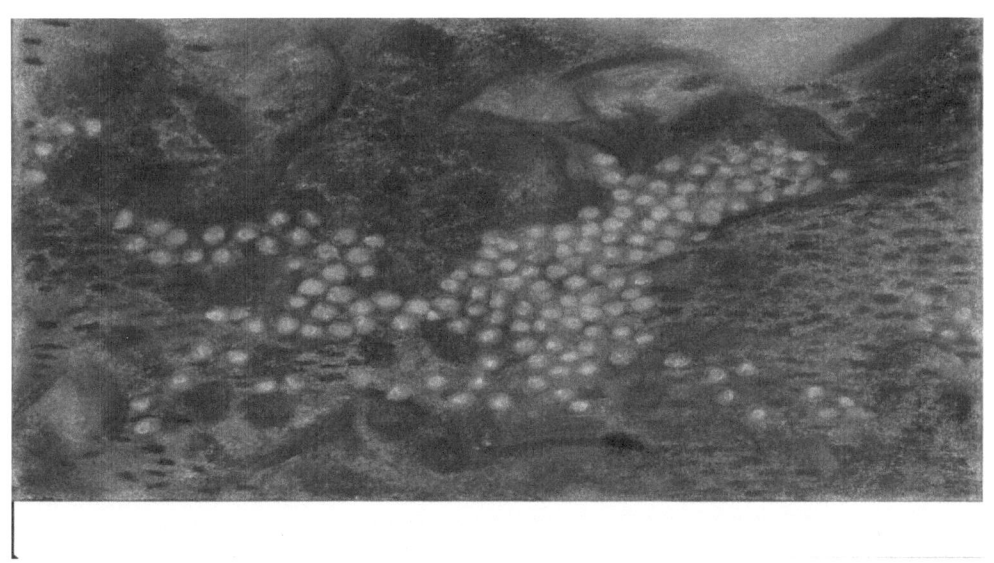

"Splish splash, no.
My eggs are hidden in the water under stones. Just in case anyone tries to eat them for lunch to put fat on their bones." said Mrs Trout.

When he got to the other side he pulled himself onto the bank, holding onto a big branch. He didn't want to slide back in case the egg and the leaf sank.

The egg and the sack were wet so he took them off his back and rolled the egg on the springy grass
to dry.
Suddenly there was a
BUMP!
And an
OUCH!
He heard someone cry.

It was Mrs Hedgehog. She was very shy. She had curled into a prickle ball and began to roll away. She didn't want to speak to Pooka at all.

"Stop please" called Pooka. He picked up the egg and put it back in the dock leaf sack on his back.

She stopped and said "What do you have in that sack on your back?"

"A speckled egg, shiny and blue. Is it yours? Is this where it grew? Said Pooka.

"Bristle, bristle, no.
I don't lay eggs. I have four or five spikey babies.
I hide them in a nest in the park. Just in case anyone wants them for dinner
When it gets dark."

So on Pooka walked when Mrs Ladybird came flying by with black and red wings out-
stretched to the sky. She flew round Pooka's head as she said.
"What do you have in that sack on your back?"
"A speckled egg, shiny and blue. Is it yours? Is this where it grew?" said Pooka.

"Flutter, flutter, no. I lay my eggs on a plant stem. Just in case anyone wants to eat them for breakfast, they grow covers so no-one can see them." said Mrs Ladybird.

Then she flew off fast in a circle and left poor Pooka in a such a spin he couldn't remember where he'd been.

BOING1

He bounced right into the big sticky web that Mrs Spider had spun. It stretched from one tree to another and Pooka couldn't tell where it begun.

"What do you have in that sack on your back?" said Mrs Spider
"A speckled egg, shiny and blue. Is it yours? Is this where it grew? Said Pooka

"Busy dizzy, no. I lay hundereds of eggs hidden in yellow silk in one big ball. Just in case any-one wants them for supper , I'm sure no-one will find them at all."

Pooka skipped on his way and nearly tripped over Mrs Snake who was slithering past.

"What do you have in that sack on your back?" said Mrs Snake.

"A speckled egg, shiny and blue. Is it yours? Is this where it grew? Said Pooka.

"Hissss, hissss, no. I lay my eggs in a big pile of manure, where it's dark and warm. Just in case anyone wants them for dinner. They won't look in there I'm sure." said Mrs Snake.

Pooka carried on. He was not in a hurry but along came Mrs Mouse she was all of a scurry.

"What do you have in that sack on your back?" said Mrs Mouse

"A speckled egg, shiny and blue. Is it yours? Is this where it grew? Said Pooka

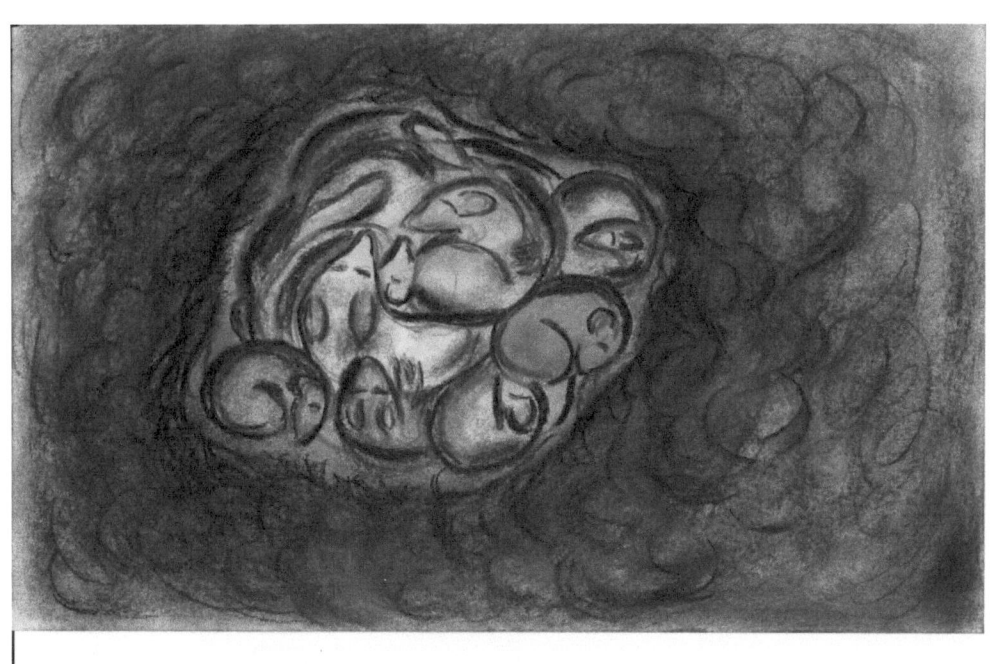

"Squeak, squeak, no. I have many babies, huddled together in a nest. Just in case anyone wants to eat them for a snack, I hide them, safe and warm, sleeping back to back." said Mrs Mouse.

Pooka found a sandy trail and there he met Mrs Snail.
"What do you have in that sack on your back? Said Mrs Snail.
"A speckeld egg, shiny and blue. Is it yours? Is this where it grew? Said Pooka

"Oh go slow no. I lay my eggs in holes in the earth. Just in case anyone fancies a treat. They stay there safely until my babies hatch and go looking for their own food to eat." said Mrs Snail.

Pooka went a little further on. The sack was starting to rub Pooka's back, making him itch and squirm. He turned a corner and found Mrs Sparrow looking for a worm.

"What is in that sack on your back?" said Mrs Sparrow."

"A speckled egg, shiny and blue. Is it yours? Is this where it grew? Said Pooka.

"Chirp chirp, no. I lay my eggs high up in a tree, just in case anyone wants to eat them for their tea. They are warm and safe in a nest except maybe from one pest.
I have one big blue baby, he looks very different from the rest and if he doesn't get all the food he goes into a very bad mood. I don't think he is one of my brood" said Mrs Sparrow.

So on Pooka walked .Pooka's legs grew tired and the egg was getting heavy. When all of a sudden he slipped and slid flat on his belly all the way down a narrow dark hole and he came face to face with Mrs Mole.

"What do you have in that sack on your back? Said Mrs Mole
"A speckled egg, shiny and blue. Is it yours? Is this where it grew? Said Pooka

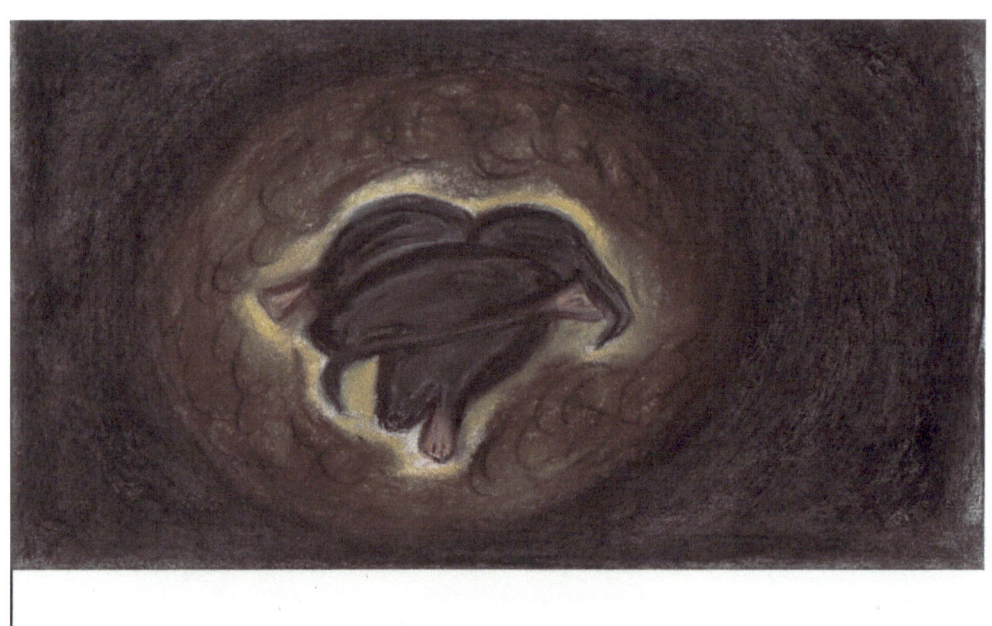

"Dig, dig, no. I have a few babies and we stay together in a long black tunnel. Just in case any-one wants them for desert, I am sure they won't find them under the dirt." said Mrs Mole.

Pooka began to climb out of the hole but all the dirt made it hard work. He got to the top but his legs began to flop.   Back down, down ,the hole he fell.

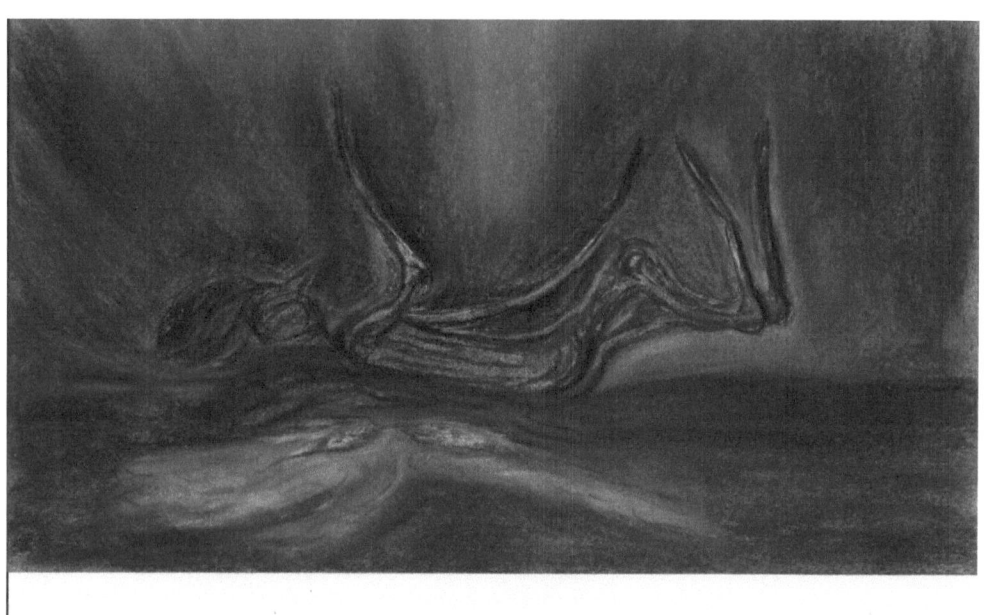

The heavy egg and the dock leaf sack made him topple right onto his back.
He heard a loud KER-ACK! And there was a horrible smell and a thick yellow goo.
The speckled egg, lay in the dirt.
OH NO, it was broken in two.

It smelt really bad and Pooka was sad.
He never did find out where the speckled egg grew.

Maybe he should have asked Mrs Cuckoo to give him a clue.
Then he remembered Mrs Sparrow who had an odd baby that was blue.
IT WAS MRS CUCKOO
She was the big pest that pushed out one of Mrs sparrow's eggs so she could lay her
own egg in someone else's nest.

www.ingramcontent.com/pod-product-compliance
Lightning Source LLC
Chambersburg PA
CBHW041531280526
45792CB00004B/1456